Digital Ecosystem Leadership

Leading From a Position of Influence, Not Authority

Overcoming Obstacles to Technology Integration

Matt Brady

DIGITAL ECOSYSTEM LEADERSHIP

Digital Ecosystem Leadership

Leading Technological Change & Overcoming Obstacles to Technology Integration From a Position of Influence, Not Authority

Regional Technology Coordinator
Technology, Learning and Instructional Coach
Information Literacy Specialist
Educational Integration Specialist
Instructional Technology Manager
Educational Technologist
Director of Assessment and Accountability
Technology Trainer
Director of Learning Technology
Academic Technology Teacher
Head of Learning Innovation
Instructional Leader for Technology
Digital Literacy Resource Teacher
Director of Digital Learning
Instructional Technology Resource Teacher
Elementary Technology Director
Director of Educational Technology
Instructional Designer
Team Leader and iPad Integration Specialist
Coordinator of Instructional Technology
Director of STEM Innovation and Education
IT Adoption Manager/ Educator
District Digital Learning Team Member
Director of Technology and Information Systems
Digital Integration Specialist
Instructional Technology Resource Coach
Instructional Strategist for Technology Integration
School Improvement and Innovation Specialist
eLearning Trainer and Evangelist
Application & Integration Specialist
Technology Department Chair
Assistant Superintendent of Educational Services
Technology Instructor
Director of Digital Instruction and Technology
Digital Learning Designer
Cyber School Coordinator

Curriculum & Technology Coordinator
Tech Integration Specialist
Ed Tech Specialist
Tech Professional
Tech Coach
Instructional Technology Facilitator
ICT Integrationist
Instructional Technology Coach
Technology Integration Coordinator
Technology Integration Facilitator
Technology Coach
Blended Learning and Data Coordinator
Head of Digital Literacy
Director of Instructional Technology
Director of Innovation and Technology
21st Century Skills Integration Strategist
Learning Technologies Coach
Teacher Resource Specialist for Technology
Instructional Technology Resource Coach
Digital Learning Coach
District Technology Coach
Coordinator of Digital Learning
Innovation Specialist
Coordinator of District Technology
Tech TOSA
District Technology Integration Professional
Technology Trainer
Director of Professional Development
ICT Senior Manager
Instructional technology resource teacher
eLearning Coordinator
Tech Support Liaison
Systems Administrator
Media and Educational Technology Instructor
Technology Integrator & Educator
Technology Teacher

Matt Brady

LEAD TECH CHANGE

For Karin

Whose support and love made this work possible.

SECTION 3

Foreword

The intent of this work is to share my personal view of the technology integration challenges often faced in traditional educational settings as experienced by thousands of technology professionals, staff and students in schools around the world today. This work describes prevailing patterns in the schools I have worked in, data from academic research and feedback from peers working in similar environments. It is not concerned with stories of the great successes many schools have had integrating technology, which are told enough. What follows is a focused, critical overview with an eye toward helping others toward solutions when school leadership has failed or is incapable of reforming itself.

Feedback is welcome. E-mail to mpbrady8@gmail.com

SECTION 4

Introduction

Educational technology programs often struggle because technology integration challenges today largely stem from people/organization problems, not "technology" problems. School administrators and the (technical as opposed to educationally trained) ICT network administration teams they lead, repeatedly fail to recognize this; adding yet another layer of disconnect between their decision making and the classroom. Those with the actual knowledge to design effective classroom integration programs- staff, integrationists, coaches, coordinators, etc.- are too often not a part of the leadership team and do not have the access or decision making influence to do what they do best.

This book contains a blueprint for initiating and sustaining technological change from positions of influence only, outside of a school's core leadership team. It identifies the common causes and effects of ineffective integration programs and lays out the leadership principles and obstacle avoidance strategies needed to empower others to use technology effectively for teaching and learning. My hope is that these insights and examples will serve as a helpful guide as you take action to lead technological change.

Matt Brady

July 2017

CHAPTER 1

Getting Beyond PB & J

The way educational technology
leadership is approached today is akin
to expecting crops
to grow without farmers, only
sharecroppers and migrants

SECTION 1

Process

"Why hasn't educational technology transformed learning in the majority of the schools who have spent untold billions on IT?"

Educational technology programs aren't delivering significant returns on investment because the real challenges around educational technology have nothing to do with the technology itself. We have the tools, the platforms, the connectivity, and devices needed to succeed today. Today's technology is far less confusing and doesn't require the frequent tweaking and fixing of a type that required more technical skill than most people had, or cared to acquire in the past.

Reviewing the research and literature on technology integration, one finds that it is often characterized as being "long on hope and hype and short on reports of outcomes that might be judged worthwhile." Most often cited are the struggles to establish new technology in the classroom and the difficulty in continuing the use of the technology over time.

Many of the chronic problems plaguing technology implementations in schools can be traced back to well meaning leadership in over their heads as to how to setup and run a successful technology program. Academic research generally cites the lack of positive outcomes being a result of unsuccessful administration-led forced integration projects. Technologies are thrust into classrooms and teachers are required to incorporate technologies for which they may not have much understanding or interest. They found that teachers who were required to find useful things to do with technology tools often instead fabricated or marginalized usage.

Hierarchical authority, as it is in schools tends to evoke compliance, not foster commitment, yet we know there is no substitute for commitment in bringing about deep change. No one can force another person to learn if the changes involve fundamental new ways of thinking and acting. Leading Learning Organizations (MIT Center for Organizational Learning Research Monograph), (Cambridge, Mass.: MIT Center for Organizational Learning, 1995).

Copyright © 1995 by Peter M. Senge

The successful integration of educational technology in a school hinges on school administrators' technology leadership abilities in fostering commitment, not demanding compliance. While schools have plenty of administrative infrastructure for decision making, they often lack administrative capacity for learning, especially around technology. It is unbelievable how similar/common the problems in schools are given the endless amount of ink spilled on designing and implementing school technology programs.

We can safely assume at least a few, if not many of these descriptors fit your technology programs now or at some point in the past: (Note: they have little to do with "technology" itself.)

Your devices came first before a solid training framework was in place

Wild variance in staff/student technology proficiency

Lip service paid to technology but minimal administrative support

Technology implementations and solutions are out of alignment with needs

Your vision and goals sound fantastic on paper, but few solid systems are in place to reach those goals

There is little or no measurement of achievements/progress

Lack of training time

No technology curriculum that the students follow

Poor technology coordinators

General distrust of technology having a positive impact on student learning

Veteran teachers would rather retire than learn to integrate a new technology

Teachers not being held accountable by their direct reports

Not having a technology

integrationist to support teachers

With so many witnessing these type of results, how can it be that school integration programs are so similar? Three key features feed the cycle of mediocrity:

1. Leadership team members who don't understand technology to any reasonable degree leading ICT departments

2. ICT departments who aren't trained/suited to meet the wide variety of needs of staff and students in an education environment

3. Organizational surveys and committees focusing attention on “telling” leadership what is wrong that do nothing to encourage individual accountability and tend to reinforce the mind-set that only top management has the power to fix problems

SECTION 2

Bureaucracy & Suboptimization

When teams fail, it's usually not because they don't have great ideas. It's because they aren't including the people who have them.

When it comes to Technology, administrative leadership often treats it like the typical education fad: five to ten year rotation of what's “in”. As if Technology is just lip-service they have to pay towards this seasons buzzword/concept like “group work”, or “differentiated learning” (now formally debunked) or flipped classrooms or “everything will be better if all the desks are in rows.”

To get “IT” going, administrators are often very good at devising or leading the development of “cargo cult” plans and goals that work fine as accreditation verbiage but aren’t the real systems, processes and resources that make an educational technology program actually work. The thinking seems to be that if you cargo-cult a technology-infused culture long enough, having it all written neatly in the handbook will somehow transform your school environment one bullet pointed goal at a time.

With so many cargo cult installations, what prevents growth in integration is in large part the animosity generated during implementation as the two groups most often responsible (administration and IT departments) often struggle with understanding and empathy toward classroom conditions and/or grapple with broken processes and politics.

The job of school leadership is to grease the wheels by providing teachers with the resources, time and guidance to try things and to share what they've learned with colleagues. If you asked your average teacher what words came to mind when considering the technology programs handed down to them from their administration; ample resources, time, guidance and sharing are not top concepts that most staff would offer up.

Suboptimization @ the IT Department

IT department personnel often report feeling as though administration doesn't fully respect their mission despite almost every system in the school depending on IT.

A common complaint from IT managers is that IT appears on administration radar in two typical ways: 1) when something breaks, and 2) when the budget is revisited and interest in IT cuts are reinvigorated.

IT departments uphold the never-ending mission of reducing the cost of moving data, being "compliant" with standards and keeping devices and facilities working. They provide many services that are often treated as commodity product; having wifi, email, file storage, calendars, etc..As such, IT often gets treated as a product, not a service, where the focus gets placed on boxes/features instead of benefits. This product focused attitude is the default mindset for ICT staff as they often sleep/eat/breathe technology and quickly forget that teachers do not.

This results in sub-optimized systems that are often designed for the way IT people assume staff and students are or they think they should be— not the wildly diverse bunch they actually are. There is a pervasive stereotype of the "surly" IT guy; smug, not always helpful, condescending, lacking empathy. I've seen and worked with both IT department personnel who fit the stereotype as well as IT personnel who helped others consistently with patience, kindness and compassion. Which ones you have in your school make a world of difference, and for the most part, it's not the "IT guys" who are to blame for sub-optimized systems.

That IT departments are almost always accountable to a leadership team that doesn't understand how to measure the effectiveness of its work to any reliable degree also contributes to the sub-optimization problem. Qualitatively dismal performance from ICT staff is tolerated because leadership is convinced "IT has to be done this way" and the "IT guys" are the only ones that can run the "technology".

It is critical to note that the growth of "software as a service" and the use of cloud apps/storage has replaced much of the specialized work IT departments have traditionally been responsible for. The wide adoption of G Suite in schools, for example, can and has reliably replaced many of the services IT departments have traditionally provided. It is possible/common that G Suite is administered by a tech savvy teacher alone.

A common metric administrators ask It personnel to about is "How many help desk tickets are open?", when the more important metric is "How are those help desk tickets being answered?" Leadership often have a skewed perception of thinking everything is fine because the ICT staff jumps when their boss says they have a problem, but have no idea that staff and students are receiving an altogether different level of service and responsiveness. The lack of a service-minded orientation on the part of IT staff only serves to reinforce the harmful “compliance vs. commitment” that follows from administration lead, top down technology initiatives. Some common sub optimizations in IT include:

Systems put in place as “product” enforce compliance, don’t consider what quality is.

Changes and feature implementations done without consultation with groups it wIll affect.

The core network connections, signups, usernames and passwords aren’t designed for access, effectively bottlenecking the entire thing before it starts.

Solutions often don’t map back to needs and create accessibility challenges for students. So many programs make massive investments and forget that the control layers added in schools by IT departments reduce the usability factor to a huge degree.

IT departments fighting against the nature of the customers vs modifying their approaches and the extreme: “this particular thing doesn't matter because I don't need it. And because I don't need it, nobody needs it at all"

Which leads to ICT staff regularly denying

needed service and materials for priorities. "I don't need another charge cable yet for my iPad, why should Teacher X?" Forgetting the massive differences in asking someone to use equipment in a commercial fashion, versus personal use.

As with any other group. tribalism within IT departments is powerful and it gets in the way of effective integration as working in school is about teamwork, majority-building and addition — adding more and more people to your coalition. Clannishness, by contrast is about tight and exclusive bonds; it's an approach based on loyalty and a tensely personal and feud-ridden way of being. In even a moderately supervised service field, the lack of empathy, followup or proactive service very commonly cited with IT support departments simply wouldn't cut it.

Hand-holding beginners can be one of the best services a community can provide, and it can go a long way to growing a community. That doesn't mean everybody needs to be teacher/mentor/educator; it's just best that those who don't want to be aren't put out front to lead. It is deeply unfair for all involved that school administration continue to put IT professionals whose core strengths are in hardware and software ill-trained for close support/training and service to students and staff.

SECTION 3

Jams & Conways Law

If experimentation and competition are suppressed to protect vested interests, the system rots from within.

Technology and education is often steeped in profoundly political processes where turf battles over power and control create conflict and resistance. The result of process and bureaucracy norms is- jams.

The way to get ahead in many schools is to

excel in naysaying and jamming, but do so while proclaiming your undying support of innovation. Innovation is fine as a principle, of course, but once it threatens vested interests- which it always does- it's quickly sent to the "further study is needed" graveyard.

When naysayers and their jams rule, the system stagnates. Stagnation leads to a decline in vitality and the ability of the organization to solve problems. Naysayers feel they're performing a valuable, even heroic duty in shooting down solutions. It's easy to think of reasons why something won't work. It requires an insanely small amount of effort compared to finding a way to make something work. "Reasons why not" are a dime a dozen. Even though you were hired for your expertise and ability to understand subtleties and edges of the Technology integration challenge, you will have all manner of other influencers who will want to come in with their all purpose hammer and turn everything into a nail.

Naysayers think that foolish people who might otherwise take unwarranted risks are saved from themselves thanks to their efforts.

People naysay to protect their pay, perquisites, position and social standing from the threat posed by new solutions. Experimentation and competition are threats to vested interests, and we all understand the motivation to protect our share of the pie from the threat posed by faster, better, cheaper. If experimentation and competition are suppressed to protect vested interests, the system rots from within as it can't iterate fast enough or in many cases, cannot change at all.

It's not accidental that "naysaying organizations" are centralized hierarchies, and the authoritarian structure of schools have well known limitations. However, there is another interesting feature of the jams that result from organizational design, identified in the late 1960s by Mel Conway.

Conway's law

"Organisations which design systems are constrained to produce designs which are copies of the communications structures of those organisations" Mel Conway, 1968

The law is based on the reasoning that in order for a software module to function, multiple authors must communicate frequently with each other. Therefore, the software interface structure of a system will reflect the social boundaries of the organization(s) that produced it, across which communication is more difficult.

There are several different ways to

understand the effects that follow from this law (originally applied to the software industry) as it occurs in schools.

No system can be better organized than the team that creates it. So, if it is known that your school has communication problems internally, then you are constrained such that your school will produce a system that has similarly inefficient or ineffective architecture for communication *externally*.

Certain types of organizations can't deliver certain kinds of systems. Most often, the structure of a system reflects the status and power relationships of the people and organizations involved. Thus, an organization's structure mirrors the internal concerns of the organization rather than the needs of the users. Once organized this way, the inertia is hard to break no matter who or what is served by that mode.

In healthy organizations, the gap between vision and reality is what creates creative tension that drives programs forward. Too often in schools where bureaucratic jams and Conway's law are in full effect, however, leadership has every incentive to reduce this tension, push reality under the rug and gloss over a programs shortcomings. Telling the truth about what is cared about is the core of leadership, but too often the incentives for leadership aren't in alignment with the kinds of things that transform education. When this is the case, there is no genuine trust or curiosity to get to the potentially embarrassing information that might cause real change.

In other words, everyone being wrapped up in process, bureaucracy and jams retards a school's technology vision from becoming a reality.

Embracing new structures and improving the corporate culture, especially communication, prior to the design of a new system can improve its success as much or more than devoting more resources to the design and implementation team. The way you improve school culture and communication is to be the change you wish to see.

CHAPTER 2

Baking PIE Into Your Program

"You never change things by fighting the existing reality. To change something, build a new model that makes the existing model obsolete."
Buckminster Fuller

SECTION 1

Leading A Digital Learning Ecosystem

Innovation is all about the formation and exploitation of new patterns. To become successful as innovators, we need to be able to step back from the existing patterns that surround us every day and start looking at them from completely fresh perspectives. We must find ways to surface and overturn the flawed assumptions, the comfortable orthodoxies and the erroneous core beliefs that may be locking us into one way of thinking and blinding us to new possibilities.

We need to notice staff and student needs and frustrations that are currently unaddressed. We need to notice the paradigms and practices that deserve to be challenged. Simply put, we need to start noticing the patterns to which we may have formerly been blind or the leadership has been blind to.

We are at a place similar to when technology integrationists first emerged in schools except now integration requires a broader and deeper player added to meet the expectations placed on tech given how heavily many schools rely on technology to undergird both administrative and classroom functions. The interdependence on IT is now too large to be handled by non-specialist leadership making pronouncements from mountaintops.

While it is true that more and more schools are deploying teachers as technology integrationists and IT coaches, far fewer have IT Directors on their leadership teams working to bridge the overlapping power centers between Principals, IT departments and staff and students.

The Digital Learning Ecosystem

As stated earlier, what is commonly

referred to as “Technology” in a school is actually a sociotechnical system, an interlinked, systems based mixture of people, technology and their environment.

The role of leadership in technology integration is to be the ecologist for the organization. Integrationists learn how to see the school as a system and to see it as a system within the context of the larger systems of which it is a part. Generating, capturing and sharing useful insights requires that one see this larger system. It is not “Technology”, it is your digital learning ecosystem. Only when seen from this perspective can we create a productive environment for our students and staff that reliably provides return on investment.

Absent this holistic understanding of all the forces at play, you won't be able to develop the capabilities in others to create the outcomes you want.

One of the true challenges of technology integration is leading from a position of influence not authority.

When someone with little or no positional authority begins inquiring to see which people are genuinely interested in changing the way they and their teams work, the only ones likely to respond are those who are genuinely interested. And if the internal networker finds one person who is interested and asks, "Who else do you think really cares about these things," he or she is likely to receive an honest response. The only authority possessed by internal networkers comes from the strength of their convictions and the clarity of their ideas. This, we find time and again, is the only legitimate authority when deep changes are required, regardless of one's organizational position. The internal networkers have the paradoxical advantage that this is their only source of authority.

"What matters is that effective internal networkers are seen as credible, knowledgeable, committed individuals who are not a particular threat to anyone. The limitations of internal networkers likewise are not difficult to identify. Because they do

not have a great deal of formal authority, they can do little to directly counter hierarchical authority. If a local line leader becomes a threat to peers or superiors, they may be powerless to help her or him. Internal networkers have no authority to institute changes in organizational structures or processes. So, even though they are essential, they will be most effective in concert with local line leaders and executive leaders." Peter Senge

In short, you must get the attention if not access to he leadership team if you don't have positional authority, otherwise you're leaving real organization-wide technology integration on the table.Working hard to develop a better understanding about how things are changing, planning the appropriate strategic responses, giving ownership to your teams and taking responsibility for outcomes is how you close the gap between today and tomorrow.

To do this, you need to leave process, bureaucracy and jams (PB &J) behind and become known for PIE: Professionalism, Insight and Execution.

SECTION 2

Professionalism

Professional leadership is not a rank nor a title. It is a choice to prioritize the well-being of those directly responsible for a school's success first.

Prioritizing means:

Setting unambiguous, measurable and clear goals. Communicating the vision back to your team/community. Buy in necessitates that the process be credible, trusted and believable.

Constantly assessing problems proactively and developing strategies and systems to help others work around bottlenecks and deficits.

Providing comprehensive support that exceeds expectations.

Providing ample opportunity to give/receive feedback.

Professional leadership in tech integration has little to do with selling others on new apps with whiz bang features. It's selling the benefits of good days: a teacher wowing their students with great lessons, staff reclaiming personal time through less time spent marking or helping a teacher reach ALL of their students. It is a commitment to continuous improvement and enthusiasm for problem solving evident to everyone you work with. Leading by example and maintaining a service orientation in everything you do is how you inspire those around you to do the same.

By asking users to embrace — or at least tolerate — new values, new skills, new behaviors, new expectations and new aspirations the best leaders get others to want to improve on their own. Your job isn't just assisting others to do something technologically different; you're assisting your colleagues in *becoming someone different.*

SECTION 3

Insight

Insight means understanding the real problems staff and students have. They might be simple and basic to where focusing on encouraging further innovation and incorporating new capacities/technologies doesn't fit personal teaching and learning needs.

Apps are a dime a dozen, they all file/save/cut/paste/delete/share, you just have to know where to look for the buttons.

What's scarce today is not the ability to find and use apps; what's scarce is the insight in how to optimize for your environment.

I'd trade any amount of app, device or platform knowledge for 1/4 of an amount of cultural insight. i'll trot out my little adage again stated a bit differently: technology integration is largely a marketing problem, not a technology problem. You need to be able to convince people to move forward. Understanding the problems in your ecosystem first and build things that support your marketing activities around the solutions to those problems, rather than building tech that you hope you can find a market for.

This means providing resources for ALL staff and students by focusing on accessibility and personalized learning. It means inspiring teachers to try new tools and strategies by making their current systems to organize, instruct & inspire work first before integrating anything "extra". Underneath it all is a commitment to providing service and communication systems that don't undermine people's sense of competence.

SECTION 4

Execution

Remember, most staff care somewhere around 0% about the technologies you're using as long as they are getting the value you promised them. What you are really integrating is the benefits of technology: You’re selling good days; for example, the ability of a student to extend their learning at their own pace.

What are some of the strategies you need to use to effectively execute for students and staff?

Don't pretend to be a wizard that can't be bothered with "simple, silly" questions.

Make sure that anything new is announced well in advance, questions answered promptly, fears addressed immediately.

Run a zero inbox- nobody leaves work without hearing from you if they sent you something before end of day.

Don't chase trends and expect others to constantly be trying new things, etc..

Do what you say you are going to do so staff trust you.

Constantly connect departments for collaborative projects.

Lobby administration to get and keep all communication systems technologies open and functioning optimally to help make staff lives easier/faster using technology so they know what is possible when IT is done right.

Be personable and form personal relationships with everyone in the school. Knowing background on each user, what they do with IT, their strengths and challenges is the key to effective support. Knowing background on users comes from being a keen observer of pain points: notice a messy desktop, a convoluted workflow, or other minor details.

Use peer led training and departmental and team teaching so everyone has someone they can learn with and can see other “non-tech” people “doing IT” successfully.

Accept criticism: be willing to examine your methods and change them based on staff feedback.

Remain willing to expend great amounts of energy even in the face of repeated resistance.

SECTION 5

PIE Examples

STUDENT LEARNING and STAFF SUPPORT

Matt Brady
Digital Ecosystem Design

- Analytics, Data and Surveys to Influence Policy
- Cultural Change: Listening and Empowerment
- Capacity Building: Student Leadership

I create digital ecosystems that transform and inspire.

Problem solving, system creation and support across cultures and environments, online and off.

Overview

I took a Technology program that teaching staff were heavily disappointed with and improved it by changing the conversation from one about iPad apps, features and functions to one about users, systems and teaching and learning

Background

Surveys after hiring in showed that staff ranked the "information systems" at the school the most unsatisfactory component of their workplace. Generally speaking, the cause was a sub optimization problem, whereby the Technology implementations and solutions were out of alignment with actual teaching and learning needs. Staff also reported that too often Technology got rolled out untested, missing functionalities and without adequate provision made for training

The result was a digital ecosystem that left needs unmet and undermined people's sense of competence, thereby creating animosity, bottlenecks and hampering growth

Challenges

- ICT staff with no experience in an educational setting having difficulty assisting users
- Technology solutions optimized for "security and privacy" often didn't map back to needs and created accessibility challenges for students
- A focus on "Technology" without the training necessary for staff to gain the knowledge of how to put it all together to perform usefully
- Lack of Student and Staff voice in decision making regarding Technology
- Teaching Assistants were not included in Staff IT training and given the worst computers yet their workloads involved the digital-media-centric work most in need of a good machine and the latest knowledge of time-saving workflows
- There was no formalized, effective IT curriculum/training time allotted in the Primary or Secondary schools beyond piecemeal efforts in various classes

Solutions

- Increased the operational effectiveness of ICT staff by helping them to understand and embrace changes in practice needed in educational setting
- Rolled out Google Apps for Education to improve our ability to discover, connect and interact with each other across institutional boundaries
- Used Google Analytics to identify trends in technology use, site traffic and staff/student needs
- Collected staff feedback on existing processes for usability and readability and then implemented their feedback/solutions or delegated to others
- Overcame objections from the ICT department to bring in Google Chrome to fit the workflows appropriate for and desired by teachers and students
- Built BIS Extra Curricular programs to expand opportunities for students including livecasting and a technology program to nurture student interests in STEM subjects and connect them with community organizations

What I did

- Turned user needs into project goals and seeds of an IT vision
- Put teaching and Learning first in system design and integration
- Brought in Google Apps for Education for collaboration, user friendly workflows and data driven accountability
- Modeled an open, transparent style of empathetic IT support & collaborative problem solving
- Setup systems for personalized learning
- Built partnerships with the BIS community
- Created a coach booking solution to make support simple

Benefits

- Improved ROI on technology investment
- Made both teaching and ICT staff happy by bringing them closer together
- Empowered staff and students by making support and training available 24/7
- Let leaders lead from any chair
- Increased numbers of staff moving further along the SAMR spectrum
- Engaged the whole community

SYSTEMS INTEGRATION and TRAINING

Matt Brady

Digital Ecosystem Design

- Integration Planning & Development
- Staff Training & Digital Competence
- Digital Literacy Resources for Students K-12

I create digital ecosystems that transform and inspire.

Problem solving, system creation and support across cultures and environments, online and off.

Overview:

I lead the shift from Technology implementation to integration by creating systems, workflows and training vehicles to set and solidify best practices toward redefinition along the SAMR (Substitution/Augmentation/Modification/Redefinition) scale

Background

In 2014, I hired in half way through a 1 to 1 iPad implementation. The program launched in 2012 with inadequate wifi coverage, a severe shortage of internet bandwidth and absent a coherent training program on the devices. Further complicating matters, the school was simultaneously embarking on a series of major administrative IT system changes swapping out its curriculum management, student database, and school website software all within the span of a calendar year

What I did

- Solved critical performance issues by listening to user feedback, uncovering problems and finding solutions
-Systems and continuous incremental improvement vs focus on devices and apps
-Worked to provide service and communication levels so that our digital ecosystem didn't undermine people's sense of competence
- Provided resources for all staff and students by focusing on accessibility, differentiation and personalized learning
- Inspired teachers to try new tools and strategies by making their current systems work like they should=

Benefits

- Setup iPads to work to their actual potential
- Reduced staff frustration
- Authentic embedding of IT
- Brought bottom 25 percent of staff to minimum digital literacy on OSX and iOS
- Improved ROI on technology investment
- Saved 25,000 euros on storage for iPads

Challenges

- Devices came first before a solid infrastructure and training framework was in place
- A set of Technology goals were cargo culted in, but the systems & processes in place to reach those goals and measurement of the program's effectiveness and achievements were superficial at best
- 200 Primary iPads were kept unsecured on floors & tables in plastic kitchen buckets
- Lack of training and relentless series of IT rollouts had staff exhausted and resentful
- When the 1 to 1 iPad program started, students had no way to upload anything other than photos and images from their iPads to ManageBac, the school's newly chosen Virtual Learning Environment
- A lack of integration assistance manpower led to iPad disuse on wide scale as the machines were constantly out of power as during initial setup, the Primary iPads were accidentally set to "never shut off." This setting, combined with the magnetic covers getting jostled in the "buckets", led to the iPads constantly turning on/being dead anytime anyone wanted to use them. This problem went unsolved for a year before my arrival
- No core IT curriculum or set aside time for basic IT literacy/training for Primary or Secondary students

Solutions

- Designed a solution for iPad storage, organized a team and built out eighteen classrooms in a weekend
- Lobbied to get dedicated ICT staff focus for the Primary school iPad program
- I found, setup and trained staff and students to use the Doc Uploads app, thereby enabling our iPad/ManageBac combination to actually work for student learning
- Rolled out Google Apps to involve and connect students and staff to improve accessibility and innovation in teaching and learning both via computer and iPad
- Created a full IT curriculum for the Primary school, Grades KG-5
- Increased staff and student voice by undertaking the largest technology surveys of staff and students in school history.
- Increased professional development and collaboration opportunities in Technology for BIS educators, TAs and other school staff
- Created minimum basic literacy self-correcting courses for staff on IOS, OSX
- Created a Primary student "Internet Drivers License" self-correcting course
- Created a Student Bulletin anyone could add to that was fully functional for iPads
- Created paperless Staff Portal substitute teacher cover and student trip lists
- Created self-tutoring resources for staff and students to master key workflows

LEADERSHIP and COMMUNICATION

Matt Brady

Digital Ecosystem Director

- Leadership by Example
- Staff/Student Engagement & Empowerment
- Service Focus for Community Satisfaction

I create digital ecosystems that transform and inspire.

Problem solving, system creation and support across cultures and environments, online and off.

What I did

- Surfaced assumptions, uncovered needs and provided safe space for candid feedback
- Took the time to understand informal networks and connected people of like minds across the organization
- Earned the trust and respect of my colleagues
- Involved many people's ideas
- Gauged support, made my case one-on-one and got things going with multiple stakeholders on board
- Introduced Google Apps for Education to support my IT vision for collaboration, efficiency, results and to support

Benefits

- New bulletin systems saved time, allowed posting flexibility, and staff learned Slides to boot
- Organization better able to move and adapt with change
- Highlighted and brought into play new values, new skills, new behaviors,, new ideas, new expectations and new aspirations that staff could relate to
- Greater autonomy/less micro-management for all

Overview

I acted on my belief that leaders can lead from any chair by setting a vision for Technology and lead the Technology program from a position of influence (no positional authority) outside of the Leadership Team

Background

BIS lacked a cohesive, shared IT vision and as a result, there were no expectations nor a coherent IT training framework for staff or students when I arrived

As the organization had no Technology Director and the Leadership Team lacked a experienced/strong voice for Technology, major sections of the school (Primary/Secondary/Early Learning, etc.) were out of sync with the others, producing inconsistency in everything from student and staff IT literacy to IT systems used

Challenges

- No coherent vision for Technology. A mishmash of goals with few provisions for the systems, execution timelines and teams to reach the goals
- IT goals consisted of cargo cult buzzwords without mechanisms for accountability or measurement of program success
- Communication standards being set by staff who don't use the systems and didn't solicit feedback from users

Solutions

- Got support and buy-in from the Leadership Team before projects started
- For every new project I assembled great teams and ensured that everyone got their voices heard, felt empowered and got time to shine/set examples
- Set a vision for Technology: to carry it out, I brought in Google Apps for Ed.
- Set minimum IT literacy baselines and designed staff communications to aid in reaching goals
- Made sure improvement of ICT service provision was prioritized equally with ICT project activity
- Started peer led trainings. Lined up commitments from people, each bringing something different to the table for personalized learning/PD sessions
- Created an environment where not being afraid to try new things and making "mistakes" was encouraged
- Built new Staff Portal systems for more efficient daily bulletins and paperless procedures for leaving substitute teaching lessons and Field Trip details.
- Created a new student bulletin process to improve communication quality and flexibility in response to student feedback
- Supported Development with Technology to showcase the school to potential new clients

CHAPTER 3

MUSIC

Successful leaders do the opposite of what typically passes for leadership: we decentralize and support

SECTION 1

The MUSIC Model

New Technology Integration Model:

PIE-PBJ= MUSIC

When you bake PIE into your

technology integration you make MUSIC:

Mediation, Usefulness, Success,
Interest, and Caring

SECTION 2

Mediation

Mediating effectively between groups fosters collaboration and ultimately shapes the culture of a school.

Being an effective mediator means you constantly work to set the proper balance between autonomy (self-reliance) and interdependence (sharing) supported by close ties and goodwill (selflessness).

Mediation is key to removing core

bottlenecks and reorganizing and setting up system structures so they are a drivers of quality rather than enforcers of compliance. Done well, it makes it harder for one group to gain control, strengthens social capital and allows the school to be able to sustain collaboration despite disagreement.

SECTION 3

Utility

The signature quality of the best school integration programs is utility, so it is important to remember that right tool for the job is often not the coolest or trendiest. Utility results when you understand why technology is useful to solve others problems and help them reach goals.

Sure, you might use your “Super Dooper New Cool Tech” to solve a problem, but the salient point is that the problem gets solved. Your staff and students don't care if you solve it with “Super Dooper New Cool Tech 5.0”, or if you solve it with a cobbled together Excel macro. They just want their problem solved.

There is certainly a time and a place to play with all the coolest and trendiest stuff, but if you're optimizing for steady growth across the organization, choosing low-risk, simple, mature tools first is the way to go. Build your technology ecosystem for your users, not for your technological pride or to demonstrate your technical prowess.

Maximizing utility often means changing the conversation from one about cool new apps and their features and functions to one about user needs, communication systems and teaching and learning. You exist to solve problems.

SECTION 4

Success

Success results when others believe if they put forth an effort they can succeed and it proceeds in identifiable stages.

Most technology users go from:

- This cannot be possible

- Awww, I’m pretty close that's incredible

- Great Scott, I’ve done it!

- Heh, I’m getting good at this

- There's no way I can screw this up

Fostering a culture of "do it yourself" then super-enabling people with great access to information along with super support logistics/fulfillment is the quickest route to success. How?

Create/launch: Build quality systems,

workflows and app combinations and get them into user hands. See what they like see what they don't. Create the conditions where students, teachers and administrators can look at evidence and share their candid perspectives back with you.

Educate/iterate: Follow launches with community wide rollout and communication with support frameworks in place. Capture feedback, figure out together how to continually improve and then make the appropriate adjustments.

SECTION 5

Interest

Interest results when others aren't overwhelmed by content and activities and things are personalized for their needs.

Your job is taking a keen interest in the success of others which in turn inspires others to expand their interest in pushing toward new milestones.

This means you need to constantly absorb new information and learn new skills. You need to be flexible, curious, trustworthy and responsive. If you are not interested in those doing or being those things, you're ability to be successful integrating technology will be limited.

SECTION 6

Caring

Caring is your ability to empathize with another human to understand his/her pain and show him/her that you care. You demonstrate caring by communicating simply and clearly. If someone understands you, they feel good about themselves. If you are talking simply and clearly, that means you have taken the time to really care about the other person.

Deep empathy and caring leads to the

discovery of innovative solutions to
important needs and problems.

SECTION 7

Coda

*If you're serving **PIE** and avoiding **PB&J**, you get **MUSIC**.*

Made in the USA
Monee, IL
05 November 2026

68030310R00052